not engaging in the rendering of legal, financial, medical or professional advice. The content within this book has been derived from various sources. Please consult a licensed professional before attempting any techniques outlined in this book.

By reading this document, the reader agrees that under no circumstances is the author responsible for any losses, direct or indirect, which are incurred as a result of the use of information contained within this document, including, but not limited to, errors, omissions, or inaccuracies.

Table of Contents

Introduction

It is a good idea to try something new each day to get out of your comfort zone. Maybe daily takeout's have been your life but try testing recipes for a chance to find out whether you have been cutting yourself from advantages. There is no need to do unique things every day. Just by applying different approaches to your daily activities, slowly over the course of time, you can change your life for the better. This book is just what you need to switch from takeout to homemade meals.

Though none of the recipes are difficult and all of them are easy to manipulate and make, cooking in the kitchen will steadily improve your skills. Sometimes, our motivation drains out if we are working hard on something that we don't want. These restaurant meals can give you the drive to continue with this learning process by providing you with a happy meal.

Cooking and food are one way to bring family and friends together and spend time with each other. There should be a family meal at least once a day. Improve your family meals and inspire other members to join you in your new hobby.

You can invite multiple friends and enjoy their never-ending compliments on your dish as well.

Good luck and Happy Cooking!

Chapter 1. Essential (Most Common Ingredient and Tools)

1. Basic kitchen equipment

Appliances

These appliances provide the greatest comfort and versatility in the kitchen:

• **Electric Mixer** - The portable hand mixer works well for all recipes in the book.

• **Blender** - This kitchen helper instantly reduces time by mixing, chopping, and pureeing food.

• **Deep Fryer** - The small Fry Daddy is best suited for controlling the temperature of cooking oil when deep-frying meat or vegetables.

• **George Foreman Indoor Grill** - This saves a lot of time in the kitchen when grilling any meat as both sides cook at the same time.

• **Microwave** - No matter how ubiquitous you are, you can count on quick defrosting and heating work in your kitchen.

A good chef knows that a good quality set of knives can achieve more in the kitchen than any electronic device. You will need these knives:

• Wide, conical chef's knife that can be easily pushed over the ingredients.

• Bread knife with serrated edges perfect for cutting through crusts.

• The peeling knife has a short blade used for peeling, cutting, seeding, and sowing vegetables.

Cooking in the kitchen can be fun, but it's the venue for potential accidents. There are some basic safety rules you need to follow to make your cooking experience more enjoyable: You should not walk barefoot in the kitchen; It is important to understand your tools and how to handle them properly. Read the instructions for using the device.

Other tools

Other tools needed to prepare food include:

• Bottle opener

• Can opener

- Filter

- Cutting board

- File

- Forks, spoons, and spatulas with long handles

- Meat seal

- Pizza cutter

- Rolling pin

- Set of measuring cups

- Measuring spoon set

- Set of mixing bowls

Cooking utensils

You will also need the following pieces:

- Frying pans with lid (small, medium, and large)

- Stockpot (big enough to make soup for your family)

- Cast iron pan (for use in the oven)

- 12-inch nonstick pan

- Baking dish

Remember these essential cakes:

- Baking plates

- Casserole dishes (small, medium, and large)

- Muffin pan

- Rectangular flat cake shape

- Roasting pan

- Pizza pan

Chapter 2. Breakfast recipes

2. Egg in a Basket

It is commonly prepared by cutting a circular or square hole in the center of a piece of bread. The bread, sometimes buttered prior to cooking, is fried in a pan with butter, margarine, cooking oil, or other fat. When browned, the bread is flipped, and the egg is cracked into the "basket" cut into the toast.

Preparation Time: 5 minutes

Cooking Time: 5 minutes

Servings: 1

Difficulty Level: Easy

Ingredients:

- Sourdough bread (1 slice)

- Margarine/butter (1 tbsp.)

- Egg (1)

- Salt & black pepper (As desired)

Directions:

Heat a skillet using the medium temperature setting. Use a small biscuit cutter to prepare the bread.

Spread butter on both sides of the bread and arrange in the pan.

To prepare an over-easy egg, toast the bread and drop the cracked egg into the ring as soon as you put the bread into the pan.

Otherwise, cook for about a minute before flipping the bread over onto the other side. Cook until the egg is the way you like it.

Nutrition

- Calories: 567

- Protein: 14.9g

- Carbs: 56.4g

- Fat: 15.6g

- Fiber: 3.6g

3. Fried Apples

These juicy, sweet apples are like apple pie filling... but better. We love them straight out of the skillet or served with a big scoop of vanilla ice cream for dessert. They're even great for breakfast—try a spoonful on top of your morning oatmeal or french toast.

Preparation Time: 10 minutes

Cooking Time: 20 minutes

Servings: 10

Difficulty Level: Easy

Ingredients:

- Butter (3 tbsp.)

- Golden Delicious apples (2 lb./4 medium)

- Granulated sugar (.25 cup)

- Brown sugar (2 tbsp. - tightly packed)

- Nutmeg (.25 tsp.)

- Cinnamon (1 tsp.)

- Apple cider (.5 cup)

- Cornstarch (1 tbsp.)

- Also Needed: 12-inch skillet

Directions:

Melt the butter using the medium temperature function on the stovetop.

Core and slice the apples into ¾-inch wedges.

Add in the apples, sugars, and spices into the skillet, stirring to coat.

Put a top on the skillet and set a timer to cook for 11-14 minutes until it's tender. Stir the mixture occasionally.

Empty the apple mixture into a serving dish and place a plastic film or foil over the top of the dish to keep it warm.

Whisk the cornstarch and cider in a small cup and stir it into the same skillet using the medium temperature setting.

Simmer the mixture until thickened or for about 30 to 60 seconds. Dump the mixture over the apples before serving.

Nutrition

- Calories: 534

- Protein: 24.3g

- Carbs: 43.5g

- Fat: 136g

- Fiber: 12g

Chapter 3. Breakfast Recipes Part 2

4. Sweet Potato Pancakes from Cracker Barrel

This Sweet Potato Pancake Recipe creates a fluffy pancake full of flavor. ... These Sweet Potato Pancakes leave those rubbery, tasteless pancakes desperate to be drowned beneath butter and syrup.

Preparation Time: 12 minutes

Cooking Time: 19 minutes

Servings: 8

Difficulty Level: Easy

Ingredients:

- One cubed sweet potato

- Half cup of milk

- Three eggs

- A quarter cup of flax seeds

- Half cup of oats (grind to flour)

- Half tsp. of baking powder

- Two scoops of protein powder (vanilla)

- A large-sized banana (sliced)

- Two teaspoons of pumpkin pie spice

- Two tbsps. of coconut oil (use as required)

- Two and a half tbsps. each of -

- Walnuts

- Pecans

- Almonds

Directions:

Take a clean pot and fill it up with fresh water. Let the water boil and then stir in the cubed sweet potatoes. Cook for a minimum time of seven-ten minutes so that the sweet potatoes become tender enough. Drain the water.

Next, you need a fork and a small bowl for mashing the potatoes.

Once your mashing is done, mix eggs, a cup of mashed sweet potatoes, oat flour, milk, flax seeds, protein powder, baking powder, pumpkin pie spice in a medium-sized bowl. After mixing evenly, stir in almonds, walnuts, pecans, and banana slices until the batter is well combined.

Now it is time to melt the coconut oil using a skillet on medium heat. For making a four-six inch thick pancake, pour the required amount of batter into the skillet. Flip the pancake once. Cook each side for three-five minutes until it is golden brown.

Nutrition

- Calories: 240.5

- Protein: 15.5g

- Carbs: 19g

- Fat: 12.4g

- Fiber: 4g

5. Waffles from Waffle House

Whether you live in a state without a Waffle House or just want to recreate their food at home, you can't have a copycat Waffle House meal without an at-home interpretation of their signature waffles.

Preparation Time: 45 minutes

Cooking Time: 30 minutes

Freezing Time: 9 hours

Servings: 6

Difficulty Level: Medium

Ingredients:

- One-fourth tsp. of vanilla

- One-fourth cup of buttermilk

- Half a cup of milk

- Half a cup of half and half

- Two tbsps. of shortening

- Two tbsps. of softened butter

- Half cup plus one tbsp. sugar (granulated)

- One egg

- Half tsp. baking soda

- One tsp. salt

- One and a half cups of all-purpose flour

Directions:

At first, take a medium-sized bowl and add baking soda, salt, and flour in it. Stir them for combining.

Take another medium-sized bowl, and beat the eggs lightly. Add the shortening, butter, and sugar and then mix them well with the help of an electric mixer until they become smooth. Then add the buttermilk, milk, half and half, and the vanilla. Then mix them well.

Then to this mixture, add the flour mixture and beat. Mix them well until smooth. Then cover it and allow it to chill overnight. (You can also use it right away, but letting it chill for 12 hours makes it much better).

Take a waffle iron and then coat it lightly with vegetable oil. Take out the batter from the refrigerator and while it is warming up a bit, preheat the waffle iron.

Spoon one-third to half a cup of batter into the preheated waffle iron. Allow it to cook for three to four minutes until the waffles turn light brown.

Note: If you really want the best results, then you should let the batter chill overnight for approximately 12 hours in the fridge. The restaurants also do this. If you cook up those waffles on the same day, even then, the recipe works just fine. If you do not want to let it cool for 12 hours, then at least, after preparing the batter, allow it to rest for about fifteen to twenty minutes so that it can thicken a little.

Nutrition

- Calories: 291

- Carbs: 33g

- Protein: 8g

- Fat: 14g

Fiber: 0g

Chapter 4. Brunch recipes

6. Cheesy Stuffed Sausage Bread

This bread features mozzarella cheese and sausage stuffed into rolled pizza dough and baked for an easy brunch, appetizer, or main meal!

Preparation Time: 20 minutes

Cooking Time: 15 minutes

Servings: 12

Difficulty: Medium

Ingredients:

- Johnsonville Mild Italian Sausage (2 pkg./1 kg.)

- Red pepper flakes (as desired)

- Italian seasoning (1 tsp.)

- Salt and pepper to taste

- Green pepper (1 diced)

- Large white onion (half of 1 - diced)

- White mushrooms, sliced (12 medium to large)

- Pizza sauce (398 ml./13.5 oz.)

- Large French loaf of bread

- Mozzarella cheese (3-4 cups)

Directions:

Fry the sausage with the pepper flakes, salt, black pepper until browned.

Remove the sausage from the pan, leaving in about one tablespoon of the drippings or one tablespoon of olive oil.

Sauté the green pepper, onion, and mushrooms until softened.

Add the sausage back in and the pizza sauce. Simmer it for about ten minutes with a lid on it. If it is too thin, let it reduce with the lid off.

Meanwhile, slice the loaf in half and pull out some of the middle of the bread.

Place the hot sausage mixture in the two halves of the bread.

Top with lots of cheese and broil it until melted. Slice and serve hot.

Nutrition

- Calories: 241.2

- Carbs: 13.1g

- Protein: 14.7g

- Fat: 6g

7. Chicken & Shrimp Carbonara

Sautéed seasoned chicken, shrimp, and spaghetti tossed in a creamy sauce with bacon and roasted red peppers.

Preparation Time: 20 minutes

Cooking Time: 40 minutes

Servings: 6

Difficulty Level: Easy

Ingredients:

- Chicken breast halves (1 lb.)

- Olive oil - divided (4 tbsp.)

- Minced garlic - divided (3 tbsp.)

- Italian seasoning (2 tbsp.)

- Jumbo shrimp (1 lb.)

- Linguine pasta (16 oz. pkg.)

- Smoked bacon - diced (8 slices)

- Onion (1 diced)

- Heavy whipping cream (1.5 cups)

- Egg yolks (4)

- Parmesan cheese (1.5 cups - grated)

- Salt & ground black pepper (1 pinch/to taste)

- Sauvignon Blanc wine (.25 cup)

Directions:

Peel and devein the shrimp and dice the bacon. Discard the bones and skin from the chicken. Chop it into bite-sized pieces.

Prepare a skillet to warm one tablespoon of oil using the med-high temperature setting. Cook and stir chicken with one tablespoon of garlic and one tablespoon of Italian seasoning (6-8 min.). Dump the chicken into a bowl for now.

Warm one tablespoon garlic and one tablespoon olive oil in the same pan. Fry the shrimp until it's a pinkish-red on the outside and white on the inside (6-8 min.). Place it with the chicken.

Add water to a large pot and wait for it to boil. Add the rest of the oil (two tablespoons). Cook the linguine until it's al dente (10-12 min.). Dump it into a colander to drain.

Toss the bacon into the pan to cook until it's just crispy, not crunchy (6 min.). Drain on two paper towels. Sauté the onion in the bacon grease until translucent (about 5 min.).

While the onion is sauteing, mix the cream, parmesan cheese, egg yolks, salt, pepper, and rest of the Italian seasoning in a mixing bowl.

Pour wine into the pan with the onions. Increase the temperature setting and wait for it to boil. Simmer it until the wine is mostly evaporated (about 2 min.). Add the creamy egg mixture and reduce heat. Simmer until sauce begins to thicken (3-5 min.). Add the chicken and shrimp; mix to coat. Serve on top of a platter of pasta.

Nutrition

- Calories: 123.2

- Carbs: 32.1g

- Protein: 23.7g

- Fat: 12.3g

Chapter 5. Starters & Entrees recipes

8. Loaded Hash Brown Casserole

Cracker Barrel offers this variation of their hash brown casserole only during certain times of the year, but with this recipe, you can enjoy it anytime you get a craving.

Preparation Time: 10 minutes

Cooking Time: 20 minutes

Difficulty Level: Medium

Servings: 4

Ingredients:

- 1 pound sausage

- 3 tablespoons chopped red bell pepper

- ½ cup grated American cheese

- ½ cup grated sharp cheddar cheese

- ½ cup grated Monterey Jack cheese

- 1½ cups grated Colby cheese (divided)

- 2 tablespoons butter

- 2 tablespoons flour

- 2 cups milk

- 2 pounds frozen hash browns

Directions:

Preheat the oven to 350°F.

Cook the sausage in a large skillet over medium-high heat while breaking it into bite-sized pieces.

Add the red pepper and cook. Drain any grease and set aside.

Melt 2 tablespoons of butter in another skillet. Stir in the flour and let it cook for a minute or so until it starts to brown. Whisk in ¼ cup of the milk and continue to cook and stir until the mixture thickens. Then whisk in the remaining milk and cook a bit longer. It will thicken up again; when it does, add the cheeses, reserving 1 cup of the Colby cheese for the top of the casserole.

In a bowl, combine the hash browns, the cheese sauce you just prepared, and the cooked sausage. Mix so that everything is combined, then pour into a baking dish and top with the reserved Colby cheese.

Cook for about 45 minutes or until the cheese is melted and the casserole is bubbly.

Nutrition:

- Calories 135

- Protein 25

- Carbs 16

- Fat 5

Chapter 6. Main Courses Recipes

9. Tuscan Garlic Chicken

With this copycat recipe, you can have this Olive Garden

quality meal in about 45 minutes.

Preparation Time: 15 minutes

Cooking Time: 30 minutes

Servings: 6

Difficulty Level: Medium

Ingredients:

Chicken

- 1 cup all-purpose flour

- ½ cup panko bread crumbs

- 1 tablespoon garlic powder

- 2 teaspoons Italian seasoning

- 1 teaspoon sea salt

- ½ teaspoon ground black pepper

- ½ teaspoon dried basil

- ½ teaspoon dried oregano

- 3 boneless skinless chicken breasts (or 6 cutlets)

- 2 tablespoons olive oil

Pasta

- 1 pound fettuccine

Sauce

- 2 tablespoons unsalted butter

- 4 cloves garlic, minced

- 1 red bell pepper, cut into 2-inch-long thin strips

- ½ teaspoon sea salt

- ¼ teaspoon paprika

- ⅛ teaspoon ground black pepper

- 2 tablespoons all-purpose flour

- 1 cup low-sodium chicken broth

- 1 cup milk

- ½ cup half and half

- 2 cups fresh spinach, roughly chopped

- 1 cup freshly grated parmesan cheese

Directions

Preheat oven to 400°F. Line a baking sheet with parchment paper.

In a bowl, mix together flour, breadcrumbs, garlic powder, Italian seasoning, salt, pepper, basil, and oregano. Coat the chicken by tossing it in the mixture.

Heat the olive oil in a large skillet over medium heat. Carefully place the chicken in the oil. Sear for 2–3 minutes or until golden brown, making sure not to lose any of the coating.

Place chicken onto a baking sheet and then into the oven for 15–20 minutes. While the chicken is baking, cook the fettuccine according to package instructions.

To make the sauce, melt the butter in a large skillet over medium-low heat. Add the bell pepper and cook for 3–4 minutes. Season with salt, pepper, and paprika, then add the garlic and sauté for about 1 minute.

Whisk in the flour, then slowly add the chicken broth, milk, and half and half. Bring the heat to medium and simmer.

Add the spinach and cook until wilted. Let the sauce thicken and then mix in the parmesan cheese.

Remove from heat and stir until smooth. Place onto fettuccine and toss together.

Slice the chicken and place it in the fettuccine. Serve with extra parmesan cheese if desired.

Nutrition:

- Calories: 340

- Carbs: 25g

- Fat: 14g

Protein: 56g

Chapter 7. Mains

10.   Wendy's Mexican Chocolate Chili

Adapted from the old recipe that my mother used for family gatherings, because you make it in a Crock Pot ®, it's easy to get to a party. It's tasty, and I promise everyone's going to ask for this recipe.

Preparation Time: 15 minutes

Difficulty Level: Medium

Cooking Time: 2 hours 30 minutes

Servings: 6

Ingredients:

- 1 pound of ground round

- 1 cup of chopped onion

- 1 cup of hot water

- 2 (14.5 oz) cans of diced tomatoes with garlic, undrained

- 1 (15 oz) can of kidney beans, rinsed and drained

- 1 (15 oz) can of black beans, rinsed and drained

- 1 (14.5 oz) can of whole kernel corn, drained

- 1/3 cup of semisweet chocolate chips

- 2 teaspoons of chili powder

- 1 tablespoon of ground cumin

- 1/2 teaspoon of dried oregano

- 1 teaspoon of salt

Directions:

Combine the ground round with the onion in a large saucepan over medium-high heat. Cook, stirring, for about 5 minutes, until beef is browned.

Transfer the cooked beef and onion to a slow cooker. Stir in water, tomatoes, kidney beans, black beans, maize, chocolate chips, chili powder, cumin, oregano, and salt. Cook on High until the chili starts to bubble for about 20 minutes. Reduce heat to low and cook for about 2 hours until thick.

Nutrition:

- Calories: 276 Cal

- Fat: 7.9 g

- Carbs: 37.3 g

- Fiber: 8 g

- Sugar: 6 g

- Protein: 16.4 g

- Cholesterol: 25 mg

- Sodium: 978 mg

11. Wendy's Mild Mannered Chili

I like chili, but for the sake of heat, I'm not a fan of heat. I wanted something that was going to warm me up but not be overwhelmingly hot, and that was the result. My husband says this would make a good sloppy Joe (with beans) as well.

Preparation Time: 15 minutes

Difficulty Level: Easy

Cooking Time: 3 hours 5 minutes

Servings: 10

Ingredients:

- cooking spray

- 1 pound of ground turkey

- 1 (28 oz) can of crushed tomatoes

- 1 (15 oz) can of black beans, rinsed and drained

- 1 (15 oz) can of kidney beans, rinsed and drained

- 1 (14.5 oz) can of diced tomatoes

- 1 (6 oz) can of tomato paste

- 3 tablespoons of chili powder

- 2 teaspoons of ground black pepper

- 1 teaspoon of salt

- 1/2 teaspoon of garlic powder

Directions:

Coat the inside of a slow cooker lightly with a cooking spray.

Heat up a large skillet over medium-high heat. Cook the ground turkey in the hot skillet until browned and crumbly, for 5 to 7 minutes; drain and discard the grease. Transfer the ground turkey to the slow boiler.

Stir the ground turkey with crushed tomatoes, black beans, kidney beans, diced tomatoes, tomato paste, chili powder, black pepper, and salt and garlic powder.

Cook on the low side for 3 hours.

Nutrition:

- Calories: 197 Cal

- Fat: 4.4 g

- Carbs: 25.4 g

- Fiber: 8 g

- Sugar: 6 g

- Protein: 16.5 g

- Cholesterol: 33 mg

Sodium: 838 mg

Chapter 8. Side Dishes recipes

12.Chocolate Indulgence Cake

Butter, eggs, sugar, and flour. That's all you need to transform bittersweet chocolate into this decadent chocolate cake. No frosting necessary!

Preparation Time: 15 minutes

Cooking Time:30 minutes

Difficulty Level: Challenging

Servings: 24

Ingredients:

- 8 oz. semisweet chocolate

- 2 ½ sticks unsalted butter, softened

- 6 eggs, separated

- ¼ cup strong espresso coffee

- 1 cup granulated sugar

- ⅓ cup cornstarch

- 1 teaspoon baking powder

- 1 cup ground almonds

To serve

- whipped cream

- cocoa powder

Directions:

Set the oven's temperature to exactly 350 degrees F for preheating;

Take a 10-inches baking pan and oil it with some melted butter;

Set up a double boiler and add butter and chocolate to its bowl;

Cook the chocolate in the boiler until it is completely melted;

Stir in espresso and mix well with the chocolate. Remove the mixture from the heat;

Leave the mixture for 5 minutes and allow it to cool;

Meanwhile, take a large mixing bowl and add the sugar and egg yolks;

Beat the ingredients using an electric mixer until smooth and fluffy;

Stir in almonds, baking powder, and cornstarch; mix well;

Gradually add chocolate melt and mix until well incorporated;

Beat the egg whites in a separate bowl using an electric beater until it makes stiff peaks;

Add the whisked egg whites to the chocolate mixture and stir gently until completely incorporated;

Spread this batter in the prepared pan and bake it for 30 minutes in the preheated oven;

Once baked, insert a toothpick to check the cake, it should be a little sticky;

Leave the cake on a wire rack and allow it to cool for 10 minutes;

Slice and garnish each slice with whipped cream and cocoa powder;

Serve.

Nutrition:

- Calories: 345

- Carbs: 23g

- Fat: 13g

- Protein: 12g

13. Chocolate Oreo Cake

This Oreo Chocolate Cake is layers of moist, homemade chocolate cake filled with a creamy Oreo frosting and topped with more crushed Oreos.

Preparation Time: 20 minutes

Cooking Time: 33 minutes

Difficulty Level: Moderate

Servings: 24

Ingredients:

- 2 cups flour

- 2 cups sugar

- ¾ cup unsweetened cocoa powder

- 2 teaspoon baking soda

- 1 teaspoon salt

- 2 large eggs

- 1 cup buttermilk

- 1 cup of vegetable oil

- 1 ½ teaspoon vanilla extract

- 1 cup boiling water

Oreo Icing

- 1 ½ cups butter

- 1 ½ cups shortening

- 8 cups powdered sugar

- 3 cups Oreo crumbs

- 1 teaspoon vanilla extract

- 7 tablespoon water

Directions

Set the oven's temperature to exactly 300 degrees F for preheating;

Take three 8-inches cake pans and grease them with cooking spray and layer them with a parchment sheet. Keep these pans aside;

Take a large-sized bowl and add flour, sugar, cocoa powder, baking soda, and salt. Mix these dry ingredients together;

Take another bowl and add eggs, buttermilk, vegetable oil, vanilla extract, and water. Beat the dry ingredients into the egg mixture until smooth and lump-free;

Divide the batter into the three cakes pans and allow the batter to set;

Place the 3 pans in the oven and bake it for 33 minutes in the preheated oven;

Once baked, remove the cakes from the oven and allow them to cool on a wire rack;

Meanwhile, beat butter with shortening and sugar in a mixing bowl using an electric beater;

Stir in half of the Oreo crumbs and vanilla; mix gently;

Add remaining water and sugar; mix until smooth and thick;

Place one cake on the serving platter and top it with ⅓ of the icing;

Set the other cake on top of the frosting and top it with another ⅓ of the icing;

Finally, set the third cake layer on top and spread the remaining icing on top;

Garnish the cake with the remaining Oreo crumbs;

Slice and serve.

Nutrition:

- Calories: 311

- Carbs: 23g

- Fat: 32g

- Protein: 42g

Chapter 9. Sides and Salads Recipes

14.Cinnamon Apples

Cracker Barrel's fried apples are perfect sitting atop ice cream for a deconstructed apple pie, and they're equally delicious on top of pork chops or ham. With this copycat recipe, let your imagination run wild!

Preparation Time: 10 minutes

Difficulty Level: Medium

Cooking Time: 10 minutes

Servings: 3

Ingredients:

- ¼ cup butter

- ½ cup apple cider

- 1 tablespoon cornstarch

- 2 pounds Golden Delicious apples, cored, peeled, and cut into wedges

- 1 teaspoon lemon juice

- 1 teaspoon cinnamon

- ⅛ teaspoon nutmeg

- ⅛ teaspoon allspice

- ¼ cup brown sugar

Directions:

In a large skillet, melt your butter over a medium to medium-low heat. Add the apples in a single layer, then top with the lemon juice followed by the brown sugar and spices.

Cover, reduce the heat to low and allow the apples to simmer until tender.

Transfer the apples from the skillet to a serving bowl, leaving the juices in the skillet.

Whisk ½ cup of the juice together with the cornstarch in a small bowl. Turn the heat under the skillet up to medium-high and whisk the cornstarch mixture into the rest of the juices. Stir constantly until it thickens, and there are no lumps.

Pour the juice over the bowl of apples and stir to coat.

Nutrition:

- Calories 115

- Protein 35

- Carbs 26

- Fat 5

15. Coleslaw

Cracker Barrel's coleslaw is among the best out there. This copycat recipe allows you to make it at home.

Preparation Time: 10 minutes

Difficulty Level: Medium

Cooking Time: 0 minutes

Servings: 3

Ingredients:

- 2 cups shredded cabbage

- ½ cup shredded carrots

- ½ cup shredded purple cabbage

- 1 cup Miracle Whip

- 1 teaspoon celery seeds

- ½ teaspoon salt

- ½ teaspoon pepper

- ⅓ cup sugar

- ¼ cup vinegar

- ¼ cup buttermilk

- ¼ cup milk

- 4 teaspoons lemon juice

Directions:

Toss the carrots and cabbages in a large mixing bowl.

Stir in the Miracle Whip, celery seeds, salt, pepper, sugar, vinegar, buttermilk, milk, and lemon juice. Toss again to completely combine.

Refrigerate for about 3 hours before serving.

Nutrition:

- Calories 215

- Protein 35

- Carbs 26

- Fat 5

Chapter 10. Pasta recipes

16.Cheese Cake Factory's Cannelloni

Italian Cannoli Cheesecake with a quick homemade crust and ... ever had and even better than any cheesecake from the Cheesecake Factory.

Preparation Time: 1 hour 30 minutes

Difficulty Level: Medium

Cooking Time: 50 minutes

Servings: 5

Ingredients:

- 3 Eggs

- 300 g 00 flour

- For the tomato sauce

- 250 g Tomato sauce

- 1 Garlic clove

- 3 tbsp. extra virgin olive oil

- Salt to taste

For the béchamel

- 25 g Butter

- Grated nutmeg to taste

- 250 g Whole milk

- 25 g 00 flour

- Salt up to a pinch

- 1 pinch Ground black pepper

For the stuffing

- 200 g Sausage

- 100 g Parmesan cheese DOP to be grated

- 2 Medium eggs

- 300 g Ground beef

- 80 g Onions

- 80 g Carrots

- 10 g extra virgin olive oil

- 20 g Red wine

- 60 g Celery

- Black pepper 1 pinch

- Salt up to a pinch

- To sprinkle

- 15 g Parmesan cheese DOP to be grated

Directions:

For preparing the cannelloni, begin by preparing the egg pasta. In a large bowl, pour in the beaten eggs earlier and the flour.

Use your hands to knead until you get a rather uniform mixture. Transfer the mixture on the work surface and work on it until you get a smooth dough that you will give a spherical shape. Use a plastic wrap to wrap it and leave it to rest for 1 hour.

Meanwhile, take care while making the simple sauce. Pour a drizzle of oil in a pan and add garlic. Pour in the tomato puree, pepper and salt after it browns. Use a lid to cover and on a moderate heat, let it cook for 30 minutes, occasionally stirring.

In this period, also make the béchamel. In a pan, pour in the butter and allow it to melt. Add the sieved flour and use a whisk to mix quickly. Pour in the hot milk and keep stirring once you get a slightly brown roux.

Use pepper and salt to season and add the grated nutmeg. Allow the béchamel to thicken and keep mixing it. Pour it in a glass bowl and use a contact film to cover.

Now prepare the filling. Finely chop the onions, celery, and carrot and prepare the sauté. Transfer them onto a pan with a drizzle of oil and add minced meat. Crumble the sausage with your hands after removing it from its casing.

In the pan, add the sausage and stir often until everything browns. Add pepper and salt and when the meat has changed color, add the red wine. Pour everything in a glass bowl once they have cooked for at least 10 minutes.

Add the grated parmesan and eggs when the meat has cooled and mix everything well. Your egg pasta will have rested at this point. Take the dough back and divide it in half and, with the help of a dough sheeter, spread the two halves and get a thickness of about 1-2 mm and cut rectangles with dimensions of 14x9 cm from every sheet.

Blanch a rectangle of pasta for 1 minute each at a time in much slightly salted boiling water and transfer them to the tray. Where you will have put a clean cloth. You can pass them in cold water for a moment if you want in order to block cooking, but the most crucial part is laying out different rectangles perfectly minus over lapping them.

Now take care of the cannelloni stuffing. On the shorter part of the rectangle, put some filling and use wet hands to roll them. Spread a little béchamel and few spoonsful of the sauce on the pan bottom once the cannelloni are rolled up and lay the cannelloni side by side.

Use the béchamel leftovers and sauce to cover the cannelloni surface and use grated parmesan to sprinkle the surface.

In a preheated static oven, bake for 15 minutes at 180 degrees and using the grill function, bake for 3 minutes. Once fully baked, serve your cannelloni while still hot.

STORAGE

You can use a refrigerator to store your cannelloni, close it in an airtight container for 1-2 days maximum.

You can freeze them in case you had used all fresh ingredients.

ADVICE

You can pour a mixture of eggs and meat in a piping bag to facilitate the filling of your cannelloni. This will make it easier to arrange the filling on different puff pastry rectangles.

Nutrition:

- Calories: 3960 Cal

- Fat: 160.24 g

- Carbs: 378.7 g

- Fiber: 21.4 g

- Sugar: 46.74 g

- Protein: 248.4 g

17. Cheese Cake Factory's Cranberry Celebration Cheesecake

Cool and creamy cranberry cheesecake.

Difficulty Level: Medium

Preparation Time: 45 minutes

Cooking Time: 2 hours 35 minutes

Servings: 16

Ingredients:

- 1/2 cup dried cranberries

- 2 cups cake flour

- 1/2 cup ground almonds

- 1/4 cup confectioners' sugar

- 1/2 cup cold butter, cubed

FILLING:

- 3/4 cup plus 1-1/2 cups sugar, divided

- 2 tbsps. Cornstarch

- 1/4 cup cranberry juice

- 2 cups fresh or frozen cranberries

- 4 packages (8 oz. each) cream cheese, softened

- 1 tsp. vanilla extract

- 4 eggs, lightly beaten

TOPPING:

- 2 cups (16 oz.) sour cream

- 1/4 cup sugar

- 2 teaspoons Vanilla extract

- 1 cup heavy whipping cream

- 1/4 cup ground almonds

- 1/4 cup sliced almonds, toasted

Directions:

Chop dried cranberries finely in a food processor. Put in confectioners' sugar, almonds, and flour; process till incorporated. Put in the butter; pulse barely till crumbly.

Force onto the base and 1-1/2-inch up the sides of an oiled spring form pan, 10-inch in size. Put on a baking sheet. Bake for 10 minutes at 350°.

Mix cornstarch and 3/4 cup sugar in a small saucepan; mix in cranberry juice till velvety. Put in the berries. Cook and mix till bubbly and thickened. Reserve.

Whip leftover sugar, the vanilla, and cream cheese in a big bowl till smooth. Put in the eggs; whip barely till blended. Into crust, put 1/2 of batter. Carefully scoop 3/4 cup mixture of berry on batter; put the rest of the batter on top.

Let bake for forty-five minutes, lower heat to 250°, and bake for an additional of 25 minutes to half an hour or till the middle is nearly set. Mix vanilla, sugar, and sour cream; scatter on the surface. Cook for 20 minutes to half an hour or until set. Cool on a wire rack for 10 minutes. Remove the knife around the edge of the pan; cool for an additional 1 hour. Spread the rest of the berry mixture on the surface. Chill overnight.

Whip cream till firm peaks are created; fold in the ground almonds. Pipe around the cheesecake top edge; scatter sliced almonds over.

Nutrition:

- Calories: 626 Cal

- Fat: 20 g

- Carbs: 32 g

- Fiber: 2 g

- Sugar: 450.55 g

- Protein: 10 g

Sodium: 242 mg

Chapter 11. Pasta Recipe Part 2

18.Pesto Cavatappi from Noodles & Company

Start with chewy pasta and toss it with a homemade pesto cream sauce, tomatoes, and mushrooms.

Preparation Time: 5 minutes

Cooking Time: 20 minutes

Difficulty Level: Medium

Servings: 80

Ingredients:

- 4 quarts water

- 1 tablespoon salt

- 1-pound macaroni pasta

- 1 teaspoon olive oil

- 1 large tomato, finely chopped

- 4 oz mushrooms, finely chopped

- ¼ cup chicken broth

- ¼ cup dry white wine

- ¼ cup heavy cream

- 1 cup pesto

- 1 cup Parmesan cheese, grated

Directions:

Add water and salt to a pot. Bring to a boil. Put in pasta and cook for 10 minutes or until al dente. Drain and set aside.

In a pan, heat oil. Sauté tomatoes and mushrooms for 5 minutes. Pour in broth, wine, and cream. Bring to a boil. Reduce heat to medium and simmer for 2 minutes or until mixture is thick. Stir in pesto and cook for another 2 minutes. Toss in pasta. Mix until fully coated.

Transfer onto plates and sprinkle with Parmesan cheese.

Nutrition:

- Calories: 637

- Fat: 42 g

- Carbs: 48 g

- Protein: 19 g

- Sodium: 1730 mg

Chapter 12. Soups recipes

19. Potato Soup

If you have never tried it, Cracker Barrel's potato soup is simply delicious. This copycat recipe gives you the knowledge to make it at home.

Preparation Time: 10 minutes

Cooking Time: 40 minutes

Servings: 2

Difficulty: Easy

Ingredients:

- 3 pounds potatoes, diced into ½×1-inch pieces

- ½ pound celery, chopped

- 2½ quarts water

- 4 ozs low-sodium chicken base

- ½ teaspoon pepper

- 1 tablespoon salt

- 1½ quarts skim milk

- 4 ozs margarine, melted

- 1 cup all-purpose flour

- Salt and pepper to taste

- Croutons for serving

Directions:

Add the potatoes, celery, water, chicken base, salt, and pepper to a large pot. Simmer for 20 minutes.

Add the milk and continue to cook.

Melt the margarine in a small bowl, then whisk in the flour until smooth. Add the mixture to the soup pot while whisking. Simmer for an additional 20 minutes or until potatoes are tender.

Taste and adjust seasoning with salt and pepper.

Top with a few croutons if desired and serve.

Nutrition:

- Calories: 281

- Total Fat: 30g

- Carbs: 32g

- Protein: 71g

- Fiber: 0g

Chapter 13. Lunch

20. Beef Stew

Warm up with one of our comforting beef stew recipes. Choose from slow-cooked beef casseroles, stroganoffs, or beef bourguignon for a winning family meal.

Preparation Time: 60 minutes

Cooking Time: 30 minutes

Difficulty Level: Moderate

Servings: 4

Ingredients:

- Stewing beef - medium-sized chunks (1 lb.

- Vegetable oil - divided (3 tbsp.)

- Salt and pepper (as desired)

- Flour (.5 cup)

- Onion (1 chopped)

- Medium potatoes (4)

- Carrots (5)

- Beef broth (1-quart)

- Ketchup (.33 cup)

- Peas (1 cup)

Directions:

Cut the potatoes and carrots into chunks, after peeling them.

Whisk the flour, pepper, and salt. Add the meat, tossing to cover.

Measure and add two tablespoons of oil to a large pot to warm using a medium-high temperature setting. Brown the beef in flour (all the flour).

Stir often to brown nicely. Transfer the meat onto a platter.

Pour in the last bit of oil (1 tbsp.) and sauté the onion until translucent, scraping any browned bits from the pan.

Transfer the meat into the pan with the carrots and potatoes. Pour in the stock and ketchup. Stir thoroughly to combine.

Simmer over low heat, often stirring for 1.5 hours. Adjust the seasoning to your liking.

Add in the frozen peas just before serving. Stir to defrost and serve.

Nutrition

- Calories: 452

- Fats: 43.6g

- Protein: 38g

- Net Carb: 2.4g

- Fiber: 3g

21.Chicken & Dumplings

Chicken dumplings with ground chicken and vegetable filling. Homemade dumplings are healthy and easy to make and perfect as a light meal.

Preparation Time: 45minutes

Cooking Time: 30 minutes

Difficulty Level: Moderate

Servings: 6

Ingredients:

- Whole chicken (about 3.5 lb./1 whole)

- Carrots (5)

- Onions (2 medium)

- Bay leaves (2)

- Celery (5 stalks)

- Fresh parsley (4 stalks) or Dry flakes (2 tbsp.)

- Poultry seasoning (1 tsp.)

- Freshly cracked black pepper (.5 tsp.)

- Flour (2.5 cups)

- Baking powder (3 tsp.)

- Unchilled solid shortening or butter (3 tbsp.)

- Milk (1.25 cups)

Directions:

Prepare a dutch oven with three quarts of water (enough to cover) and add the chicken. Peel the carrots, onion, and celery stalks, all roughly chopped.

Fold in half of the parsley, the bay leaves, and the rest of the spices. Once boiling, lower the temperature setting and simmer for 45 minutes. Chop it into bite-size pieces.

Toss the chicken in the pot with three cups of stock, plus the celery, salt, pepper, onion, and rest of the carrots (all finely diced). Simmer it for another 15-20 minutes.

Sift the flour, salt, and baking powder using your hands or a pastry blender to mix in the butter until crumbly. Add the rest of the chopped parsley milk to form a soft dough.

Drop the dough by the spoonful (12)on top of the chicken mixture. Simmer the dumplings with the lid off for about five minutes.

Place a lid on the pot and simmer for another 20 minutes before serving.

Nutrition

- Calories: 539

- Fats: 24g

- Protein: 56g

- Net Carb: 2.5g

- Fiber: 4g

Chapter 14. Dinner

22.   Broccoli Cheddar Chicken

This broccoli cheddar chicken is easy to make and is the perfect dish for during the week, it takes one meal and about one hour.

Preparation Time: 25 minutes

Cooking Time: 30

Servings: 4

Difficulty Level: Easy

Ingredients:

- Boneless - skinless chicken breast (4)

- Salt & black pepper (.5 tsp. of each)

- Milk (1 cup milk)

- Cheddar cheese soup (1 small can)

- Paprika (.5 tsp.)

- Cheddar cheese (6 oz. - shredded)

- Frozen chopped broccoli (8 oz.)

- Crushed buttery crackers (1.5 cups)

Directions:

Warm the oven at 350° Fahrenheit and lightly grease a baking dish.

Sprinkle the chicken using pepper and salt, adding it to the dish.

Mix the soup, milk, cheddar cheese, and paprika. Dump about half of the mixture and broccoli pieces over the chicken.

Top with the crunched crackers and the rest of the cheese mixture.

Set a timer and bake it for 45 minutes. Serve with your favorite side dish.

Nutrition:

- Calories: 210

- Carbs: 3.6g

- Fat: 19.1g

Protein: 28g

Chapter 15. Appetizers & Snacks recipes

23.   Arancini

Adapt these arancini rice balls to your liking: add fresh herbs, sundried tomatoes, or chopped ham. You can also make the balls from leftover cold risotto.

Preparation Time: 45 minutes

Cooking Time: 1 hour 20 minutes

Servings: 6

Difficulty Level: Easy

Ingredients:

- 5 cups of chicken stock or broth

- 2 cups of Arborio rice

- 1/4 pound cooked Tuscan sausage, cartons removed,

- 1 1/4 cups of Parmigiano Reggiano cheese crumbled

- 3 eggs lightly beaten

- kosher salt

- 3/4 cup cubed fontina cheese

- 2 cups of breadcrumbs

- extra virgin oil for deep frying

Directions

Boil the stock in a deep saucepan and cook the rice until all have been cooked. Take the sausage from the heat and add the cheese. Stir in one egg, when cooled slightly. Let the mixture cool down on a platter.

Beat the remainder of the eggs in a bowl with a pinch of salt. Form the rice mixture into balls the size of walnuts using a table cubicle. Push a cube of cheese into the middle and close the mixture around it. In the beaten egg, roll each ball and cover with the crumbs of bread.

Heat the olive oil to 350 degrees in a deep heavy oven, and fry the balls deeply in lots until golden brown.

Drain and serve hot onto paper towels.

Nutrition

- Calories 430

- Total Fat 22g 34%

- Dietary Fiber 4g 16%

- Sugars 4g

- Protein 12g 24%

Chapter 16. Sauces & Glazes recipes

24. Applebee's Onion Peels with Dipping Sauce

This signature appetizer from Applebee's is the chain reaction to the overwhelming success of outback' blooming onion and chili's awesome blossom.

Preparation Time: 35 minutes

Cooking Time: 45 minutes

Servings: 4

Difficulty Level: Easy

Ingredients:

For Onion Peels:

- 1 cup all-purpose flour

- 2 Vidalia onions, large

- 1 cup bread crumbs

- 2 to 2 ½ cups milk

106

- 1 teaspoon fresh ground black pepper

- Oil for frying

- 1 teaspoon salt or to taste

For Creamy Horseradish Dipping Sauce:

- ½ cup mayonnaise

- 2 teaspoons white distilled vinegar

- 1/8 teaspoon cayenne

- 1 teaspoon ketchup

- 1/8 teaspoon dried oregano

- 1 tablespoon prepared horseradish

- ¼ to ½ teaspoon medium grind black pepper

- 1 teaspoon paprika

- 1/8 teaspoon garlic powder

- 1 teaspoon water

- 1/8 teaspoon onion powder

Directions:

For the Onion Peels:

Over moderate heat in a deep fryer or deep saucepan; heat the oil until hot.

Slice and remove both ends from the onion.

Place the onion, flat side down on your cutting board & cut in ½ down the middle. Cut each ½ into 4 to 5 wedges more.

For onion petals, separate the onion pieces & layers.

Combine the entire dry ingredients together in a medium-sized bowl.

Whisk in 2 cups milk & blend until you get a smooth batter-like consistency. If required, feel free to add more milk. Let sit until thickens slightly, for 5 more minutes, and then whisk again.

Dip each individual onion petal in the prepared batter. Gently shake to get rid of the excess batter & then carefully drop into the hot oil. Cook approximately 8 to 12 of the petals at one time.

Fry until turn light brown, for a minute or two, stirring gently.

Remove & place them on a plate covered with a paper towel to drain.

Repeat these steps until you have utilized the petals completely.

Serve with some Creamy Horseradish Dipping Sauce on the side and enjoy.

For Creamy Horseradish Dipping Sauce

Whisk the entire dipping sauce ingredients together in a medium-sized bowl; whisk well until creamy. Cover & let chill in a refrigerator until ready to use.

Nutrition:

- Calories: 1797 Cal

- Fat: 62.46 g

- Carbs: 269.25 g

- Fiber: 18.4 g

- Sugar: 118.94 g

- Protein: 43.55 g

25. Applebee's Cheese Chicken Tortilla Soup

This soup is quick, flavorful to make, and also very filling. Serve with tortillas or a warm cornbread.

Preparation Time: 15 minutes

Cooking Time: 30 minutes

Difficulty Level: Moderate

Servings: 6-8

Ingredients:

- 2 tablespoons vegetable oil

- 1 medium chopped onion

- 2 teaspoons minced garlic

- ¼ cup chopped green pepper

- 4 cups chicken stock

- 1 (15 oz) can tomato purée 1 teaspoon sugar

- 1 teaspoon chili powder

- 8 ozs Velveeta cheese, cut into 1" cubes

- ½ teaspoon salt

- 1 teaspoon Worcestershire sauce

- 4 tablespoons flour

- 10 (6") yellow corn tortillas

- ½ cup water

- 1 cup cream

- 1 pound cooked chicken

- ¼ cup nonfat sour cream

Directions:

Add oil and sauté garlic, onions, and green peppers in a large stockpot over medium heat.

Fill the pot with chicken stock, tomato purée, sugar, salt, chili powder, and Worcestershire sauce.

Allow it to boil, then lower heat and cook for 20 minutes.

Break tortillas into ¼" strips and bake for 6–8 minutes in the oven at 400 ° F till crispy.

Mix the flour and the water in a small bowl, then stir into the soup.

Stir in chicken and milk, bring to a boil, then simmer for 5 minutes.

Garnish with sour cream, cheese, and slices of tortilla into a bowl.

Nutrition:

- Calories: 8148 Cal

- Fat: 413.11 g

- Carbs: 133.49 g

- Fiber: 16.4 g

- Sugar: 69.84 g

Protein: 933.3 g

Chapter 17. Sauces and Dressings

26.   Chick-Fil-A Sauce

Chick-fil-A Sauce is an easy dipping, slightly smoky sauce with a hint of honey mustard that is perfect for dipping waffle fries, nuggets, and more.

Preparation Time: 5 minutes

Cooking Time: 0 minutes

Difficulty Level: Easy

Servings: 12

Ingredients:

- ¼ teaspoon onion powder

- ¼ teaspoon garlic salt

- ½ tablespoon yellow mustard

- ¼ teaspoon smoked paprika

- ½ tablespoon stevia extract, powdered

- 1 teaspoon liquid smoke

- ½ cup mayonnaise

Directions

Plug in a food processor, add all the ingredients in it, cover with the lid and then pulse for 30 seconds until smooth.

Tip the sauce into a bowl and then serve.

Nutrition:

- Calories: 183

- Fats: 20g

- Protein: 0

- Net Carb: 0

- Fiber: 0

27. Burger Sauce

This tangy sauce has a zip that goes well with a burger or as a fry dip. It is versatile and can be spicy or a kid-friendly sauce.

Preparation Time: 5 minutes

Cooking Time: 0 minutes

Difficulty Level: Easy

Servings: 12

Ingredients:

- 1 tablespoon chopped gherkin

- ½ teaspoon chopped dill

- ¾ teaspoon onion powder

- ¾ teaspoon garlic powder

- 1/8 teaspoon ground white pepper

- 1 teaspoon mustard powder

- ½ teaspoon erythritol sweetener

- ¼ teaspoon sweet paprika

- 1 teaspoon white vinegar

- ½ cup mayonnaise

Directions

Take a medium bowl, place all the ingredients for the sauce in it and then stir until well mixed.

Place the sauce for a minimum of overnight in the refrigerator to develop flavors and then serve with burgers.

Nutrition:

- Calories: 15

- Fats: 7g

- Protein: 0g

- Net Carb: 0g

- Fiber: 0g

Chapter 18. Desserts recipes

28. White Chocolate Raspberry Cheesecake

A show-stopping dessert that features the tartness of

raspberry and sweetness of white chocolate.

Preparation Time: 45 minutes

Cooking Time: 1 hour 20 minutes

Difficulty Level: Medium

Servings: 12

Ingredients:

- 1 chocolate cookie crust

- 2 pounds cream cheese, softened

- ¾ cup sugar

- 2 teaspoons vanilla extract

- ½ teaspoon almond extract

- 4 large egg yolks

- ⅔ cup raspberry sauce

- ¼ pound white chocolate

- 2 cups whipped cream

- Cooking spray

Directions

Line the outside of a 9-inch springform pan with aluminum foil. Spray the inside with cooking spray, then add the cookie crust.

Preheat the oven to 325°F.

In a mixing bowl, combine the softened cream cheese, sugar, vanilla extract, and almond extract using an electric mixer.

Add the egg yolks to the mixture. Mix until creamy and smooth.

Pour half of the batter into the crust. Place about ⅓ cup of raspberry sauce on top. Swirl with a table knife.

Pour the rest of the batter on top. Add another ⅓ cup of raspberry sauce and swirl again.

Fill a roasting pan with about 1 inch of water. Place the springform pan inside. Bake for 1 hour and 20 minutes or until the cheesecake is completely cooked.

Turn off the oven but leave the pan inside with the door slightly open. Let cool for about 30–45 minutes. (This avoids cracks in the cheesecake.)

Remove the cheesecake from the oven and let cool to room temperature.

Cover and place in the refrigerator to chill overnight.

Decorate the cheesecake with shaved white chocolate and whipped cream. Slice and serve.

Nutrition:

- Calories: 145;

- Carbs: 23g;

- Protein: 12g;

- Fats: 43 g;

29. Tiramisu

The Olive Garden pick-me-up cake for when you need that

caffeine boost.

Preparation Time: 30 minutes

Cooking Time: 20 minutes

Servings: 8 - 10

Difficulty Level: Medium

Ingredients:

- 3 egg yolks, divided

- ¼ cup whole milk

- ¾ cup granulated sugar

- 3 cups mascarpone cheese

- ½ pound cream cheese

- ¼ teaspoon vanilla extract

- 20–24 ladyfinger cookies

- ¼ cup cold espresso

- ¼ cup Kahlua coffee liqueur

- 2 teaspoons cocoa powder

Directions

Boil water in a medium saucepan over medium-high heat. Reduce heat and simmer.

In a medium bowl, whisk together the milk, sugar, and two egg yolks. Place in the saucepan (or you can use a double broiler). Stir frequently for 10 minutes or until the sugar dissolves. Remove from heat and cool.

In a large bowl, combine the mascarpone, cream cheese, and vanilla with an electric mixer. Mix until creamy. Add remaining egg yolk. Stir again.

In a small bowl, combine the espresso and Kahlua. Quickly dip each ladyfinger into the mixture, making sure it does not soak up too much liquid.

Place the ladyfingers side by side at the bottom of an 8×8 baking pan. Spoon half of the cheese mixture over the ladyfingers. Place more ladyfingers on top. Pour the remaining cheese mixture on top.

Using a strainer, dust cocoa powder on top of the last cheese mixture layer. Cover and chill for several hours. Slice and serve.

Nutrition:

- Calories: 123;

- Carbs: 43g;

- Protein: 25g;

Fats: 14g;

Chapter 19. Snacks

30. Cottage cheese "strawberries with cream"

It is not only the vitamin C that makes strawberries an immune defense booster: the secondary plant substances abundantly present in strawberries include many polyphenols. They are able to render germs harmless and can also help prevent inflammation.

Preparation Time: 15 minutes

Cooking Time: 45 minutes

Servings: 6

Difficulty Level: Moderate

Ingredients:

- Fat cottage cheese-800 gr.

- Semolina-5 tbsp.

- Eggs - 3-4 pcs.

- Salt-1/2 tsp

- Sugar 1/2 tbsp. (adjust to your liking)

- Vanilla

- Dried fruits (raisins or whatever you like. I have a citrus flavor, candied pamello)

For cream and filling:

- Fresh strawberries_200-300 gr.

- Fat cream (sour cream) -3-4 tablespoons

- Sugar

Directions

Wipe the cottage cheese through a fine sieve.

Blatter the eggs with sugar, salt, and vanilla, add the egg mixture to the curd, put the semolina, sliced candied fruit, mix and put into the mold, pre-greased it with vegetable oil and sprinkled with cereal.

Cut the strawberries into plates; lay them tightly on the curd dough.

Separately, prepare the cream, whip the sour cream or cream with sugar and apply the cream on the strawberries.

Bake the manna until cooked, but do not overdo it in the oven.

Nutrition:

- Calories: 145;

- Carbs: 18 g;

- Protein: 29g;

- Fats: 24 g;

31. Sand Cheese and Apple Pie

Apple Pie Grilled Cheese Is the Ultimate Sweet-Savory Comfort Food

Preparation Time: 5 minutes

Cooking Time: 20 minutes

Servings: 6

Difficulty Level: Moderate

Ingredients:

- Cinnamon – pinch

- Cottage cheese - 500 g

- An Apple - 1 kg

- Baking powder - 1 teaspoon

- Margarine - 200 g

- Sugar - 1.5 cups

- Wheat flour - 2 cups

- Sour cream - 100 g

- Chicken egg - 4 pieces

Directions

For the test, grind 3 yolks (we carefully separate them with proteins) with 0.5 cups of sugar, then grind with softened (not melted) margarine (butter), then introduce the flour, baking powder, knead a rather thick dough with your hands, finally mix in roll sour cream into a bowl, cover and then refrigerate for at least half an hour while the filling is being prepared and the oven is preheated

Rub the cottage cheese, mix with 1/3 cup sugar and 1 yolk (add the protein from the egg to the remaining three)

Peel the apples and seeds, cut into thin slices (until the dough is rolled out, it is better to sprinkle them with lemon juice or diluted citric acid so that they do not darken, but you can cut them already when the cake is ready to be planted in the oven).

Roll out the dough thin enough on a rather large baking sheet, making sides along the edges (so that the curd does not drip). We spread evenly the curd filling, beautifully lay the apple slices on it, and sprinkle with cinnamon. We put the oven preheated to 200 degrees for 30-40 minutes.

While the cake is baking, beat the whites with the remaining sugar in a thick foam.

Take out the slightly baked cake and lay the protein foam over the apples evenly, level it, and put it in the hot oven again. When in a few minutes these grab a light brown crust - the cake is ready!!!

Nutrition:

- Calories: 135;

- Carbs:15 g;

- Protein: 23.5g;

Fats: 14 g;

Chapter 20. Beverages, Drinks & Coffee recipes

32.   Hazelnut Frappuccino From Starbucks

A blend of deliciously nutty flavor, classic vanilla, and a touch of spice makes this Frappuccino anything but boring. Simple to order, yet full of flavor! Our favorite combination.

Preparation Time: 5 minutes

Cooking Time: 0 minutes

Servings: 3

Difficulty Level: Easy

Ingredients:

- Half a cup of Nutella

- Two cups of vanilla ice cream

- One cup of whole milk

- Six ice cubes

- Four teaspoons of espresso powder (instant)

For Optional:

- Chocolate curls

Directions

Use a blender for mixing Nutella, milk, and espresso powder and cover it to blend completely. Combine ice cubes and blend to make a smooth mixture.

Then mix ice cream and blend the mixture by covering it. Make sure the mixture is smooth.

Pour the prepared mixture into glasses.

Serve immediately to enjoy it.

You can garnish the mixture by using chocolate curls as per your choice.

Note: It is a delicious drink with cocoa, coffee, and nutty flavors.

Nutrition:

- Calories: 474;

- Carbs:55 g;

- Protein: 9g;

- Fats: 2 g;

33. Green Apple Moscato Sangria From Olive Garden

Have you tried the Olive Garden Green Apple Sangria made with Moscato wine? It is a delicious fall-inspired sangria that is super easy to make.

Preparation Time: 5 minutes

Cooking Time: 0 minutes

Servings: 6

Difficulty Level: Easy

Ingredients:

- Eight cups of ice

- Seven hundred fifty ml. of Moscato

- Half a cup each of

- Orange slices

- Strawberries

- Green apple slices

- Six ozs each of

- Apple puree

- Pineapple juice

Directions

Make a mixture of pineapple juice, apple puree, and chilled Moscato in a large-sized pitcher.

Stir the mixture well.

Take several ice cubes in a glass and pour the iced beverage in the glass before serving it.

Serve and enjoy it.

Notes:

If you want to have a fun drink at a festive occasion and you don't want it to contain too much alcohol, then sangria is the drink for you.

You can make it tastier by adding some slices of fruits such as blueberries, orange, strawberries, and so on.

Nutrition:

- Calories: 210;

- Carbs: 35 g;

- Protein: 0g;

- Fats: 0g;

Chapter 21. Nutritious Fish and Seafood Main Entrees

34. Seafood Alfredo

An Olive Garden's favorite for seafood lovers. A creamy, rich alfredo sauce with fettuccine with lots of shrimp and scallops that is quick and easy to make.

Preparation Time: 15 minutes

Cooking Time: 15 minutes

Servings: 5

Difficulty Level: Moderate

Ingredients:

- 1 pound fettuccine noodles

- 1 pound scallops

- 1 pound small shrimp, deveined, shells and tails removed

- ½ cup butter

- ¼ cup olive oil (divided)

- 5 cloves garlic, minced

- 1 quart heavy cream

- ¼ teaspoon black pepper

- 1½ cups parmesan cheese, shredded

- 1¾ cups mozzarella cheese, shredded

Directions:

Heat a skillet over medium-high heat. Add 2 tablespoons of the olive oil and the scallops. Sauté for 6 minutes.

Mix in the shrimp. Cook for about 4–5 minutes or until fully cooked. Remove from pan and set aside.

In a large saucepan, melt the butter with remaining olive oil over medium heat. Add garlic, cream, and pepper. Cook for 5 minutes, whisking frequently.

Add the parmesan cheese. Cook on medium heat for 10–15 minutes or until thickened, whisking often.

Add the mozzarella cheese. Stir frequently while cooking the fettuccine noodles according to package directions.

Drain the pasta and toss it into the sauce with the seafood. Mix well and serve.

Nutrition:

- Calories: 219

- Fat: 17 g

- Saturated fat: 10 g

- Carbs: 28 g

- Sugar: 7 g

- Fibers: 1 g

- Protein: 17 g

- Sodium: 1134 mg

35.   Salmon Piccata

Impress your guests with this easy but fancy Salmon Piccata copycat recipe.

Preparation Time: 20 minutes

Cooking Time: 15 minutes

Servings: 4

Difficulty Level: Easy

Ingredients:

Salmon

- 1½ pounds salmon fillets

- Lemon pepper marinade

- Lemon pepper seasoning

- 2 tablespoons butter

- 2 tablespoons olive oil

Piccata sauce

- 2 tablespoons butter

- 4 cloves garlic, minced

- ⅔ cup white cooking wine

- 2 cups chicken broth

- ½ cup lemon juice

- 2 teaspoons cornstarch

- ½ cup capers, rinsed and drained

Directions:

Trim the salmon fillets to ½ inch thickness, if necessary. Place in a Ziploc bag and pour the lemon pepper marinade inside. Refrigerate for 1 hour.

Transfer the salmon to a tray. Season with lemon pepper.

Place the butter and olive oil in a frying pan.

To make the piccata sauce, melt the butter in a saucepan over medium heat. Add the garlic and cook for 1 minute.

Add the white wine. Simmer until almost evaporated, then whisk in ¾ of the chicken broth and lemon juice. Simmer for another 4 minutes.

While the sauce is simmering, place the frying pan on the stovetop over medium heat until the butter and oil sizzle. Cook the salmon until golden brown and completely cooked.

Add the cornstarch to the simmering sauce. Continue to simmer until thickened.

Add the capers and simmer for 1 minute. Remove from heat. Drizzle sauce over salmon. Serve.

Nutrition:

- Calories: 119

- Fat: 17 g

- Saturated fat: 10 g

- Carbs: 28 g

- Sugar: 7 g

- Fibers: 1 g

- Protein: 17 g

Sodium: 1134 mg

Chapter 22. Chicken and Fish Recipes

36.   Chicken and Dumplings

Chicken and dumplings is one of Cracker Barrel's most loved recipes, and this copycat recipe now enables you to make it at home.

Preparation Time: 10 minutes

Cooking Time: 25 minutes

Servings: 4

Difficulty Level: Moderate

Ingredients:

- 2 cups flour

- ½ teaspoon baking powder

- 1 pinch salt

- 2 tablespoons butter

- 1 scant cup buttermilk

- 2 quarts chicken broth

- 3 cups cooked chicken

Directions:

Make the dumplings by combining the flour, baking powder, and salt in a large bowl. Using a pastry cutter or two knives, cut the butter into the flour mixture. Stir in the milk a little at a time until it forms a dough ball.

Cover your countertop with enough flour that the dough will not stick when you roll it out. Roll out the dough relatively thin, then cut into squares to form dumplings.

Flour a plate and transfer the dough from the counter to the plate.

Bring the chicken broth to a boil in a large saucepan, then drop the dumplings in one by one, stirring continually. The excess flour will thicken the broth. Cook for about 20 minutes or until the dumplings are no longer doughy.

Add the chicken, stir to combine, and serve.

Nutrition:

- Calories: 211

- Total Fat: 23g

- Carbs: 12g

- Protein: 81g

- Fiber: 0g

37.   Chicken Pot Pie

Want to discover a classic Southern secret? Well, this recipe is the one you need to check out. The Double Crust Chicken pot pie is enough to dazzle your guests and bring the Southern atmosphere home. The golden crust will win you over the raving analysis at the dinner table.

Preparation Time: 30 minutes

Cooking Time: 45 minutes

Servings: 4

Difficulty Level: Moderate

Ingredients:

- ½ cup butter

- 1 medium onion, diced

- 1 (14.5-oz) can chicken broth

- 1 cup half and half milk

- ½ cup all-purpose flour

- 1 carrot, diced

- 1 celery stalk, diced

- 3 medium potatoes, peeled and diced

- 3 cups cooked chicken, diced

- ½ cup frozen peas

- 1 teaspoon chicken seasoning

- ½ teaspoon salt

- ½ teaspoon ground pepper

- 1 single refrigerated pie crust

- 1 egg

- Water

Directions:

Preheat the oven to 375°F.

In a large skillet, heat the butter over medium heat, add the leeks and sauté for 3 minutes.

Sprinkle flour over the mixture, and continue to stir constantly for 3 minutes.

Whisking constantly, blend in the chicken broth and milk. Bring the mixture to a boil. Reduce heat to medium-low.

Add the carrots, celery, potatoes, salt, pepper, and stir to combine. Cook for 10-15 minutes or until veggies are cooked through but still crisp. Add chicken and peas. Stir to combine.

Transfer chicken filling to a deep 9-inch pie dish.

Fit the pie crust sheet on top and press the edges around the dish to seal the crust. Trim the excess if needed.

In a separate bowl, whisk an egg with 1 tablespoon of water, and brush the mixture over the top of the pie. With a knife, cut a few slits to let steam escape.

Bake the pie in the oven on the middle oven rack 20 to 30 minutes until the crust becomes golden brown.

Let the pie rest for about 15 minutes before serving.

Note: Alternatively, to serve it like exactly Cracker Barrel, use individual baking dishes and proceed the same way, using a homemade or store-bought crust that you can roll out will make it easier to shape the required crust for each dish.

Nutrition:

- Calories: 111

- Total Fat: 23g

- Carbs: 12g

- Protein: 81g

Fiber: 0g

Chapter 23. Favorite Copycat Recipes

38. McDonald's Sausage Egg McMuffin

Make from scratch this healthy version of your McDonald's favorite in under 30 minutes—and you don't even have to leave the house.

Difficulty Level: Easy

Preparation Time: 10 minutes

Cooking Time: 20 minutes

Servings: 4

Ingredients:

- 4 English muffins, cut in half horizontally

- 4 slices of American processed cheese

- ½ tablespoon oil

- 1-pound ground pork, minced

- ½ teaspoon dried sage, ground

- ½ teaspoon dried thyme

- 1 teaspoon onion powder

- ¾ teaspoon black pepper

- ¾ teaspoon salt

- ½ teaspoon white sugar

- 4 large ⅓-inch onion ring slices

- 4 large eggs

- 2 tablespoons water

Directions:

Preheat oven to 300°F.

Cover one half of the muffin with cheese, leaving one half uncovered. Transfer both halves to a baking tray. Place in oven.

For the sausage patties, use your hands to mix pork, sage, thyme, onion powder, pepper, salt, and sugar in a bowl. Form into 4 patties. Make sure they are slightly larger than the muffins.

Heat oil in a pan. Cook patties on both sides for at least 2 minutes each or until all sides turn brown. Remove the tray of muffins from the oven. Place cooked sausage patties on top of the cheese on muffins. Return tray to the oven.

In the same pan, position onion rings flat into a single layer. Crack one egg inside each of the onion rings to make them round. Add water carefully into the sides of the pan and cover. Cook for 2 minutes.

Remove the tray of muffins from the oven. Add eggs on top of patties, then top with the other muffin half. Serve warm.

Nutrition:

- Calories: 1155;

- Carbs: 32 g;

- Protein: 13g;

- Fats: 44 g;

39. Chipotle's Refried Beans

So many Tex Mex and Mexican dishes benefit from an appropriate smear of refried beans. With this recipe in your arsenal, we're positive you'll find many makes use of your own.

Difficulty Level: Medium

Preparation Time: 5 minutes

Cooking Time: 10 minutes

Servings: 6

Ingredients:

- 1-pound dried pinto beans

- 6 cups warm water

- ½ cup bacon fat

- 2 teaspoons salt

- 1 teaspoon cumin

- ½ teaspoon black pepper

- ½ teaspoon cayenne pepper

Directions:

Rinse and drain the pinto beans. Check them over and cast off any stones.

Put the beans in a Dutch oven and add the water. Bring the pot to a boil, decrease the heat, and simmer for two hours, stirring frequently.

When the beans are tender, reserve ½ cup of the boiling water and drain the rest.

Heat the bacon fat in a large, deep skillet. Add the beans 1 cup at a time, mashing and stirring as you go.

Add the spices and some of the cooking liquid if the beans are too dry.

Nutrition:

- Calories: 1355;

- Carbs: 32 g;

- Protein: 13g;

Fats: 34 g;

Chapter 24. Popular Copycat Recipes

40.   In N' Out Burger

Preparation Time: 10 minutes

Cooking Time: 10 minutes

Servings: 5

Difficulty Level: Easy

Ingredients:

- 1½ pound ground beef 1½ teaspoon salt

- 1 teaspoon ground black pepper 5 slices of American cheese

For sauce

- 1/3 cup mayonnaise

- 1 tablespoon unsweetened tomato paste

- 1 teaspoon mustard

- 2 tablespoons cucumber cucumber

- 2 teaspoons cucumber juice

- ½ teaspoon salt

- ½ teaspoon pepper

Directions

Prepare the sauce, take a small bowl, put all the ingredients in it, stir until mixed, discuss until needed. Prepare burrito, take a medium bowl, add the meat, add salt and pepper, stir until fully mixed, then cut the mixture into ten small balls.

Take a frying pan, heat it, grease with oil, then add the meatballs while hot, squeeze and cook on each side for 4 to 5 minutes until fully cooked and brown.

When you are finished, place a piece of cheese on the patty, stack it with another patty, and repeat the remaining steps.

Put the burgers together, use two lettuce leaves at the bottom of the bread, add a few slices of onion, cover the stacked burgers, and then cover two slices of tomato and pickles.

Spread the prepared seasoning on the patties and cover the top with two lettuce leaves.

Put the rest of the burgers together in the same way and serve.

Nutrition:

- Calories: 696;

- Carbs: 4 g;

- Protein: 52g;

- Fats: 50 g;

Chapter 25. Others

41. Wendy's Chili

Wendy's Chili Copycat Made With Kidney Beans, Onions, Chilis, Bell Peppers And Tomatoes With A Spicy Chili Powder And Cumin Spices. The Perfect Copycat!

Preparation Time: 10 minutes

Cooking Time: 1 hour 50 minutes

Servings: 8

Difficulty Level: Easy

Ingredients:

- 3 pounds ground beef

- 1 ½ cups diced white onion

- ½ cup diced red bell pepper

- 1 cup chopped tomatoes

- 2/3 cups diced celery

- ½ cup diced green bell pepper

- 1 teaspoon garlic powder

- 1 teaspoon salt

- 2 teaspoons erythritol sweetener

- 1 teaspoon cumin

- ½ teaspoon ground black pepper

- ½ teaspoon oregano

- 3 tablespoons red chili powder

- 1 ½ teaspoon Worcestershire sauce

- 15 ozs crushed tomatoes

- 1 ½ cups tomato juice

- 2 tablespoons avocado oil

Directions

Take a large pot, place it over medium heat, add oil and when hot, add beef and then cook for 10 to 15 minutes until golden brown.

Drain the excess greases, add bell peppers, tomatoes, celery, and onion, switch heat to medium-high level and cook for 5 minutes.

Add remaining ingredients, stir until well mixed and then simmer the chili for 1 hour and 30 minutes until cooked, covering the pot.

Serve straight away.

Nutrition:

- Calories: 344;

- Carbs: 2g;

- Protein: 9g;

- Fats: 21g;

- Fiber 2g

Chapter 26. Cooking Conversion Chart (volume, temperature, ...)

Measuring Equivalent Chart

Type	Imperial	Imperial	Metric
Weight	1 dry oz		28g
	1 pound	16 dry ozs	0.45 kg
Volume	1 teaspoon		5 ml
	1 dessert spoon	2 teaspoons	10 ml
	1 tablespoon	3 teaspoons	15 ml
	1 Australian tablespoon	4 teaspoons	20 ml
	1 fluid oz	2 tablespoons	30 ml
	1 cup	16 tablespoons	240 ml

	1 cup	8 fluid ozs	240 ml
	1 pint	2 cups	470 ml
	1 quart	2 pints	0.95 l
	1 gallon	4 quarts	3.8 l
Length	1 inch		2.54 cm

* Numbers are rounded to the closest equivalent

2. Oven Temperature Equivalent Chart

Fahrenheit (°F)	Celsius (°C)	Gas Mark
220	100	
225	110	1/4
250	120	1/2
275	140	1
300	150	2
325	160	3
350	180	4
375	190	5
400	200	6

425	220	7
450	230	8
475	250	9
500	260	

* Celsius (°C) = T (°F)-32] * 5/9

** Fahrenheit (°F) = T (°C) * 9/5 + 32

*** Numbers are rounded to the closest equivalent

Conclusion

These recipes are the perfect additions to your daily meals. If you want affordable restaurant-style food, then here is the answer.

We've got recipes from all your favorite restaurants—and then some. If you ever host a party, there are dishes in here that will make your guests ask, "Hey, what's the recipe for that chicken you served?" If you regularly cook for yourself or your family, then these simple recipes will help you elevate your meals. And if you just love having restaurant food at home, and then try making some yourself—you never know you might even be a better cook!

Lunch in Italy is usually served after antipasto, a common appetizer that Italians enjoy before having their main meal. Antipasto can be hot or cold. Then comes the primo piatto (first course). Soup, salad, and risotto are common choices for the primo piatto. After that may come the secondi piatto (second course), although not all Italians like to eat two courses for lunch. If served, the secondi piatto usually includes a meat or seafood dish with an optional side dish such as baked vegetables or a salad.

Dinner for Italians is an opportunity to spend quality time with their family and friends. Dinner is usually taken together with all family members to end the day on a good note. Just like lunch, it starts with an appetizer followed by one or two meal courses, which may be pasta and pizza as well as meat or seafood dishes. Pizza is usually cooked in a brick oven. Dessert is always served after dinner; however, some people also have dessert after lunch.

CPSIA information can be obtained
at www.ICGtesting.com
Printed in the USA
BVHW061246050721
611165BV00002B/348